DATE DUE

Printed
in USA

THE VALUES LIBRARY

SELF-ESTEEM

A close, supportive family gives its members a strong sense of confidence and self-esteem.

THE VALUES LIBRARY

SELF-ESTEEM

Alicia Thomas

THE ROSEN PUBLISHING GROUP, INC.
NEW YORK

Published in 1991, 1993 by The Rosen Publishing Group, Inc.
29 East 21st Street, New York, NY 10010.

Revised Edition 1993

Copyright © 1991, 1993 by The Rosen Publishing Group, Inc.

Printed in Canada.

Library of Congress Cataloging-in-Publication Data

Thomas, Alicia.
      Self-esteem / Alicia Thomas.
      (The Values library)
      Includes bibliographical references and index.
      Summary: Discusses the importance of self-esteem, how to attain it, and how to improve your life by strengthening your self-esteem.
      ISBN 0-8239-1749-5
      1. Self-respect—Juvenile literature. [1. Self-respect.] I. Title. II. Series.
BF697.5S46T46   1991
158'.1—dc20
                                       91-32973
                                          CIP
                                          AC

C O N T E N T S

INTRODUCTION:SELF-ESTEEM— RESPECT FOR OURSELVES

HAVING SELF-ESTEEM—A FEELING OF SELF-WORTH and of self-respect—means having the feeling that you are a valuable person. Your life is worthwhile. When you have self-esteem, you think of yourself as someone who is important. You feel that you deserve to reach your goals. You feel that you have what it takes to do well.

The love and caring of others can help us develop self-esteem, especially when we are very young. The fact that others see us as worthwhile makes it easier for us to believe in ourselves. But self-esteem does not depend entirely on others. You can develop and increase your own self-esteem. To do this, you need to understand what self-esteem is and where it comes from. You have to be able to see the good things about yourself.

Positive self-esteem helps you to hold your head high. You *know* who you are, and you *like* who you are. Each of us is a person who is worthy of love and respect. Everyone of us is unique. None of us is perfect. But there are things about each of us that can make us proud of who we are. Once we learn to recognize these traits, we can use them to strengthen our belief in ourselves.

This book can help you take a closer look at what makes you special. Maybe you:

- are kind and helpful to others
- look after a younger brother or sister
- do well in school, on a job, or in sports
- are creative
- are a good friend.

We all need to work on self-esteem throughout our lives. No one can expect that life will be perfect. Each one of us will have problems to solve. There will be times that will require strength and courage. Without a healthy sense of self-esteem, people may treat themselves badly. They may give up on themselves instead of trying to solve their problems. Or they may let others persuade them to make poor choices.

Many professionals who study our society believe that a lack of self-esteem is at the root of many of our serious social problems. Teens, especially, can fall victim to bad influences if they do not have healthy self-esteem. A young person who does not have a strong belief in her or his own worth is much more likely to drop out of school, become involved in crime, abuse drugs or alcohol, or take unnecessary risks.

Self-esteem is important to all of us, and there is much to learn about it. This book will help you to do that.

Self-esteem gives us the confidence we need to handle situations like job interviews.

1

WHAT MAKES US SPECIAL— ELEMENTS OF SELF ESTEEM

A HEALTHY ATTITUDE ABOUT YOURSELF—positive self-esteem— begins with an understanding of who you are. Every one of us is a special person—there are no two of us exactly alike. Even identical twins have different personalities, qualities that set them apart.

Learning to identify and appreciate our special qualities is part of growing up. And it is the foundation of self-esteem. Self-esteem is what makes us strong when we need to be strong. It makes it possible for us to find courage within ourselves. Knowing who you are, and liking yourself for who you are, helps you to get along with others. It helps you to know what's best for you, and to do your best.

No one is good at everything. But everyone is good at many things. Have you ever taken the time to think about who you are? If you tried to make a list of all the things you know about yourself, you might be surprised at how long the list would grow. You would learn something about the many ways in which people are alike and the many ways in which they are different.

Judging Ourselves

Are you outgoing? Do you find it easy to talk to people you have just met? Or are you shy, preferring to let some-one else do the talking? It isn't better to be outgoing than to be shy. Outgoing and shy are just different ways of behaving. If everyone were shy, no one would talk to anyone else. And if everyone were outgoing, it might be hard to get a word in edgewise. A person with healthy self-esteem says it's okay to be shy or outgoing. Either way you are someone others can like and respect.

When we judge ourselves without healthy self-esteem we can be much too harsh on ourselves. Our standards may be unrealistic and too demanding. We find that we fall short. A healthy sense of self, however, enables us to see things in a positive way. For example, you can think that someone is more attractive than you are, but not nec-essarily a better person. We cannot all be beautiful. And if someone gets the answers faster than you do in math class, that's okay, too. You would be able to tell yourself that being good in math isn't everything. You have other strong points, maybe writing or public speaking.

Being realistic about ourselves means seeing the things we would like to change as well as the things we are proud of. That's where positive self-esteem can be really important to us. And self-esteem can help us maintain a

Panic and self-doubt are
powerful emotions that
can keep you from
achieving your goals.

good feeling about ourselves even when we do not suc-
ceed at something we try to do.

You are still a worthwhile person even if the birdhouse
you tried to make in shop class isn't good enough to dis-
play at the school crafts fair. Before you took shop you
couldn't build anything at all. Healthy self-esteem enables
you to look at the birdhouse and be proud of yourself for
trying to learn some new skills.

Think Positive

We can increase our self-esteem by looking in a positive
way not only at the things we do, but at the ways we
behave, and the attitudes we have. Having confidence in
yourself is one of the primary building-blocks of healthy
self-esteem. Are you self-confident? Do you think of your-
self as someone who is able to succeed at a task, or
achieve a goal. Those positive feelings about yourself are
part of self-esteem.

Feeling good about yourself doesn't mean being con-
ceited. It means being proud. And pride can be helpful.
You don't have to be the smartest person in your class.
You can be proud of a good attendance record. You can
be proud of working cooperatively with your classmates
and being respectful to your teachers. If you are a good
athlete, you can be proud of your performance, and proud

of helping the team. But you can also help the team whether you are a good athlete or not. You can join the pep squad, raise money for new uniforms, or help the coach by packing the equipment for "away" games. All it takes is *knowing* that you can make a contribution that is worthwhile. And that means believing in yourself and feeling good about it, too.

Young people are often very concerned with whether or not others will like them. Girls and boys both have fears about dating—whether they will be asked out on dates, whether someone they ask out will accept. If you feel that you would not be fun to be with, you probably would not have a good time on a date. The better you like yourself, the more likely it is that others will like you. Healthy self-esteem means liking who you are.

As teens seek more independence from parents and families, they often turn to peer groups for support and a sense of identity.

2

ME MYSELF, AND THE REST OF THE WORLD

JENNY LOOKED ACROSS THE CAFETERIA at the table where Nora and her friends always sat together. They were the high school's most popular girls. They starred in the plays and decided whose pictures went in the yearbook. They wore the best clothes and went out with the best-looking guys. Nora was the leader of the pack. Nora wasn't the smartest, prettiest, or nicest of the group, but she acted like a queen, and people treated her like one.

Jenny was friendly with some of the girls who hung out with Nora. But she never really wanted to be part of the group. She called it a "clique"—a group of people who excludes other people. Jenny didn't like the way Nora bossed other people around and decided who was "in" and who was "out." She couldn't understand why Matty, who was so smart, and Jane, who was so friendly when Nora wasn't around, put up with Nora's "queen bee" act. But they seemed to care a lot about being part of Nora's private club.

Jenny's friend, Leah, cared too. She was always trying to make friends with Nora and was always getting snubbed in return. She invited Nora to her party, and Nora just said, "No thanks, I'm busy." Leah's feelings were hurt. She was even more upset when none of Nora's friends showed up at the party either. Leah knew that Matty and Jane would have come if Nora hadn't made a point of snubbing her. Leah felt unpopular, unimportant, and most of all, unhappy. Her party was ruined, even though her other friends told her that they had a great time.

"Why do you care so much?" Jenny asked Leah. "If Nora and her friends are too stuck-up to be polite, who needs them?"

"I know you're right," Jenny sighed, "but it's normal to want people to like you. They make me feel . . . like a bug."

"That makes me mad!" said Jenny. "You're not a bug, you're a person who has lots of friends and lots of good qualities. But even if you had *no* friends and *nothing* going for you, you still would not deserve to be treated like a bug! Every human being deserves respect. Nobody should let others make them feel that bad about themselves. I think Nora's a bully and her friends are afraid to stand up to her. They don't respect other people because they don't respect themselves. They're the ones with the problem, not you."

Low self-esteem often
causes people to feel
worthless if they are not
accepted by the "in"
peer groups.

Respect

Jenny knows something very important. It is the single most important lesson in learning about self-esteem. She knows that every single person is valuable. One of a kind. Worth respect. She treats other people that way, and she expects to be treated that way too. She respects herself. Her worth comes from within, from herself—not from what others think.

Leah is not so sure she's worth respect. To Leah, her worth comes from outside, from how other people see her and judge her. Leah thinks that her value as a person is based on popularity. She believes that popularity comes from how you look, how smart you are, how much money you have, what kind of clothes you wear, and other qualities that can be judged from the outside. She believes that if she is not popular, she must not be good enough. She uses the standards of other people to judge herself. That's why she assumes that she must not have much value if she is not part of the "in" clique. She feels less than human— like a "bug."

Bullies and Conformity

Nora and her friends seem very sure of themselves, but inside they are fearful. Nora is a bully, strong on the outside, weak on the inside. She bosses others around to make up for the secret fear that she's not good enough.

Her friends "follow the pack" because they, too, are inse-
cure. Even if they know that something is wrong, like
rudely snubbing Leah's party, they go along with it be-
cause they are afraid to stand up for what they believe.
This is called "conformity." To conform means to follow
everybody else, no matter what you really think and feel.

Respect for Others Starts with Yourself

You cannot treat others with respect unless you value
and respect yourself first. If you treat others badly, you
lose worth in your own eyes. Self-esteem and respect for
others go hand in hand. People who hurt and abuse oth-
ers do not have this basic understanding of human worth.
They do not value themselves or anyone else.

In our example, Jenny knows, values, understands, and
listens to her "true self." It is not what other people think
of her, nor who she thinks other people want her to be,
but who she really is. Leah shortchanges her true self by
thinking she is worth only as much as others think she is
worth. Matty and Jane turn away from their true selves by
conforming, not sticking up for their inner values. They
let Nora decide what kind of people they should be. And
Nora, who is unkind to others, does not value herself.
Remember this first rule of self-esteem: RESPECT, for
yourself and others.

There is nothing better for your self-esteem than setting yourself a goal and then achieving it.

3

GOALS AND ACHIEVEMENTS

FEW THINGS IN LIFE ARE MORE SATISFYING than achieving a
goal—setting your sights on something, deciding to go
after it, and putting in every bit of effort it takes to finally
succeed. Whether your goal is something that everybody
can see—like breaking a track record or losing 10
pounds—or a private goal—like getting along better with
your family or overcoming shyness—when you reach the
goal you feel proud to be you. It's great for self-esteem.

BUT . . . setting goals that you *can't* meet is every bit as
bad for self-esteem. Sometimes we refuse to be satisfied
with ourselves. If we succeed at something, it suddenly
seems not good enough. We keep pushing ourselves,
never reaching the goal, never letting ourselves be proud
of what we've accomplished.

The Carrot and the Stick

You've probably heard the story of "The Carrot and the Stick." In the story, the farmer makes the weary donkey move by dangling a carrot tied to a stick just in front of the donkey's nose. The donkey plods forward, trying to get a bit of that carrot. But, of course, the donkey never reaches its goal. Some people spend a lifetime treating themselves like that donkey. They think that they'll be happy and proud of themselves if only they can win the next prize. The next prize is always just a little bit out of reach. The goals that really have been reached are never quite good enough.

Perfectionism and Fear of Failing

Goals sometimes work *against* self-esteem. Jill is a perfectionist. For her, it's all or nothing: A+ perfect or total failure. Never mind that most of the class got *B's* and *C's* on that tough history test. Jill got a B+, but as far as she is concerned she may just as well have flunked.

Josh, on the other hand, is terrified of goals. He is convinced that he'll never live up to them, so why bother trying? It's not only grades and contests that scare him. It's people, friendships, and especially girls. Josh thinks he's a zilch, so he can't imagine that anybody would want to be his friend. Even if someone is friendly, Josh pulls back like a turtle in its shell.

For the perfectionist, even
the smallest mistakes can
feel like a total failure.

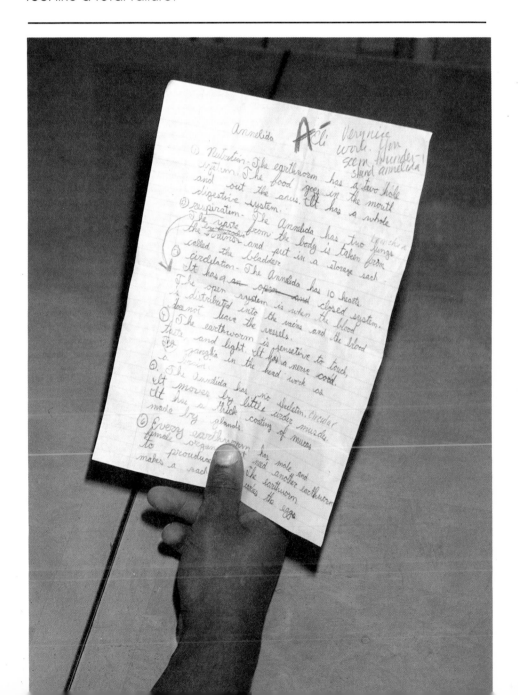

Being competitive can be a healthy way to boost self-esteem. But "winning" should not become the only way to feel good about yourself.

Both Jill and Josh are unrealistic about achieving goals. Jill thinks perfection should be within her reach. She is always disappointed and never feels a healthy sense of self-esteem. Josh is just as unrealistic. He is so ready for disappointment and rejection that he never gives himself a chance to succeed. Josh and Jill don't see things as they really are. They see *illusions.* Illusions are false ways of seeing ourselves and our world. They keep us from setting and reaching realistic goals.

How can you tell when you are setting realistic goals? It's not always easy. Take school grades, for example. Surely it is a good thing to want the best grades possible, and it's important to work hard to get them. Without that goal, you might not push yourself to get as much out of your education as you could. Getting good grades is a healthy goal. Achieving good grades can, of course, make self-esteem stronger. But education is more than good grades. And you are more than your grade point average!

To believe that better grades make you a better human being is an illusion. To be hung up on straight *A's* can be harmful to your growth and development, in education and as a person. It can cause you to have a narrow view of life and learning. You may become fearful of taking chances or trying out new ideas. Worse, if you measure your value only by grades, you are not respecting yourself as a worthy, unique person.

Competition

Competition can also work both for and against self-esteem. For example, in sports a competitive drive to win is the extra edge it takes to become a fine athlete. To want to do your best, to practice long, hard hours, to watch your performance improve, and to come out a winner is a richly satisfying experience.

But competition can also mix up self-esteem with dangerous illusions. You could start to see the world only in terms of "winners" and "losers." You could begin to feel that you must be a champ, a star, a gold medalist to really be worth anything. Reaching the top could become your whole life. We've all heard enough about the unhappy and tragic private lives of some of our greatest athletes to know that a glorious sports career doesn't always mean a glorious life.

Your Goals Are for Yourself

It's complicated. We all need goals to work toward and achievements to feel proud of. But we don't need to go through life like a donkey chasing a carrot on a stick! The answer, once again, is to know and respect yourself. Your life is not a show you put on for others. You play only one part in this show, the part of yourself, *for* yourself. If you know that you can get that C average up to a B, go for it. If you know you can shave seconds off your own best time, practice, work at it, and feel proud when you've done it. But if you know you'll never be the class valedictorian, prima ballerina, or star quarterback, what good does it do to put yourself down for it? The better you know yourself, and the more respect you have for yourself, the better you'll be at setting realistic goals and expectations for yourself. When you set real goals for yourself and then meet those goals, you'll know exactly what "self-esteem" means.

4

ENEMIES OF SELF-ESTEEM

SOME FAMILIES DEAL WITH EACH OTHER IN UNHEALTHY WAYS. They
may not provide the necessary love, care, and support that
helps children grow. A child who is born into a family
that does not meet his or her needs will have trouble
building self-esteem.

Sometimes parents or other caregivers have very serious
problems. They may be out of work for a long time.
They may be ill. They may be going through a divorce.
They may have problems with alcohol or drugs. These
parents may not have healthy self-esteem themselves.
They may not feel worthy of receiving love, and they may
be unable to show love.

Parents or caregivers who feel worthless often do things
to children that can destroy self-esteem. Physically hurting
children or neglecting them is called *child abuse*. Child
abuse is against the law.

Even Words Can Hurt

Children naturally trust their parents. They believe that
they deserve whatever their parents do or say to them.
This is why abuse can destroy a child's self-esteem. *Verbal
abuse* is as hurtful to a child as a beating. And the effects
of verbal abuse can last much longer.

Some parents don't realize how damaging and painful verbal abuse is. They may not even understand that it is abuse. But telling a child that he is stupid, or telling a child that you wish he or she had never been born, may cause far more harm than any physical blow. When children hear bad things about themselves over and over, they begin to think of themselves as bad. Abused children go through life with the sense that they are worthless and guilty of some terrible crime. Sadly, many abused children grow up to treat their own children the same way.

Harmful Messages

Most of us get through childhood without extremes of neglect and abuse. But we may still find that parents can send us confusing messages about our worth. Some parents expect perfection. They show love or give support only when a child does well. They reject the child if he or she makes mistakes. When this happens, a child learns that he or she is valuable only when the *parent's* goals are met. The child thinks that what he or she wants or feels does not matter.

On the other hand, some parents don't seem to care what their kids do. This may tell children that they are not important. At the same time, if rules and values are not passed on from parent to child, kids will be unsure of how

As an infant, your self-esteem develops as you react to the
messages you receive from your parents.

to get along with others, how to form opinions and stick to their beliefs. They will not know and respect the person they are inside.

Where to Turn?

People with low self-esteem are very vulnerable. That means that they can be easily hurt. It also means that they can get into trouble.

It's very hard to know how to think and behave in our society. Teens, especially, feel pressure from many sources. Unless teens themselves have a clear, strong set of values and beliefs, with a healthy sense of who they are, they can become confused.

Look at some of the mixed messages in our society.

- Looking out for Number One is selfish and greedy **BUT** success and winning are all-important.
- Honesty is the best policy **BUT** somebody might get mad or make fun of you if you tell the truth.
- Mature adults use reason and discussion to solve problems **BUT** "real men" use fists and guns.
- Women should be treated with respect and equality **BUT** how a woman looks is what really counts.
- Helping others is a good thing to do **BUT** nice guys finish last.
- Drugs kill **BUT** let's party.

When your self-esteem is
strong, and you feel good
about yourself, you are
able to share affection.

Teens with low self-esteem may make poor choices that can lead to serious consequences. If a young boy, for example, has little self-esteem, it may be easy for others to talk him into getting involved with drugs, or joining a gang. He may feel that no one cares what happens to him. Young girls who don't have high self-esteem may believe that they don't deserve the love and respect of their sexual partners. They could be easy targets for physical abuse. Or if a young girl feels unloved she may think about getting pregnant. For her, a baby only represents the love she needs without being judged.

Why Belief in Yourself Is Important

You have a responsibility to be the best you can be. Improving your self-esteem will help you to fight against any abuse, neglect, or other problems you may have in your life. Feeling good about yourself helps you to see things more clearly. You will be better able to:
- make decisions
- reach your goals
- accept your shortcomings
- develop healthy relationships.

It is important to understand that only with healthy self-esteem can *you* take control of your life.

Adolescence is a time when teens are searching for an adult identity and a sense of belonging.

5

THE NEED TO BELONG

WE ALL HAVE A NEED TO FIT IN. We want to belong someplace and be accepted. Self-esteem can offer you this kind of security. It can help you get through the normal disappointments, sadness, and failures in life. It tells you that you are still okay. Good self-esteem may reduce your fear because it means having a comfortable knowledge of who you are and what you can do for yourself.

Finding a Place in the World

People who have not gained a strong sense of belonging and self-worth from their families often find it hard to feel secure outside of their home. They may feel uncertain about who they are and what is right and wrong. They may always question and doubt themselves, even when things are going well. Without that sense of belonging and worth, many young people find themselves desperately searching for something that makes them feel that they matter, they are wanted, they belong.

33

If they are lucky and talented and work hard, they may find a way to matter by excelling in sports or school. They may learn to respect and esteem themselves through their accomplishments (though, as we talked about in Chapter 4, chasing goals is not always a good path to self-esteem).

Cliques

Young people often look for a sense of belonging by "following the pack," joining a clique. They dress and act just like everyone in their group. We talked about cliques and conformity in Chapter 3. Being part of a clique may give you a feeling of belonging, but following the pack without acting on your own beliefs will not build your self-esteem.

Serious Trouble

Teenagers sometimes find themselves involved in serious problems, like crime, gangs, dropping out of school, pregnancy, drugs, and alcohol abuse. These problems can often be traced back to a lack of self-esteem. Kids who have these problems are often searching for a way to belong, a way to matter.

Gangs seem to offer friendship, status, rules, structure, and a sense of belonging. Kids who have no family support or feel unloved turn to groups to find what is missing in their lives. But gangs don't solve these kids' problems.

They just make the problems worse. Gangs not only get kids in trouble with the law, they don't give kids a *real* sense of self-esteem. Kids who belong to gangs often don't think for themselves. They often are afraid to be by themselves. They feel secure or important only when they are with the others in their gang. Gangs, like cliques, destroy self-esteem.

One way that teenage girls try to find a feeling of belonging and mattering is by having a baby. A girl who feels unimportant may think that having a baby will give her a future. She will be the most important person in the world to her child. Plus, she will get attention when she is pregnant.

The reality of having a baby is something quite different. A baby demands time, attention, and money. Teenage mothers often get no help or money from their babies' fathers. School and jobs are even harder to handle; most teenage mothers drop out of school. Too often the young mother ends up trapped in poverty, lonely and bored, with even lower self-esteem. It is very hard for a teenage mother to pass on self-esteem to her baby when she feels worthless herself.

Feeling worthless also plays a part in drug and alcohol abuse and dropping out of school. School dropouts are three times more likely to be unemployed. And they are four times more likely to have been in trouble with the law as high school graduates. Girl dropouts are six times more likely to have babies and nine times more likely to be on welfare. The young person who feels worthless may turn to drinking or drugs as a way out of feeling bad. They may feel more like they belong when they are drunk or high.

Easy Solutions?

Gangs, teen pregnancy, drug and alcohol abuse, and dropping out are all big, complicated problems. There are no easy answers or quick fixes. But a stronger self-esteem helps you to avoid these traps. Schools and community groups face the task of finding ways to give children and teens a sense of belonging to our complex society. They hope to make teens feel that they matter to others. Youth groups, workshops, and counseling can help. If you are feeling insecure or you have a friend who is having trouble, go talk to someone you respect.

6

RESPONSIBILITY AND INTEGRITY

WE HAVE TALKED ABOUT HOW IMPORTANT SELF-ESTEEM IS, how we need to respect ourselves and others, and how problems inside and outside home can rob us of our self-esteem. Another major part of self-esteem is *taking responsibility for yourself.* Booker T. Washington, a black educator, said, "Few things help an individual more than to place responsibility upon him, and to let him know you trust him." This means knowing your own mind, making your own decisions, following your conscience, and acting with honor. Then you must accept the results of your decisions and actions. It means that how you lead your life is really up to you alone.

Words like *responsibility, conscience,* and *integrity* are hard to pin down. Your conscience is your set of beliefs and values that tell you what is right and wrong. Integrity means "wholeness." It means basing decisions and actions on your conscience, not on what is easy and convenient at the moment. Responsibility means living up to duties and obligations, but it also means calling the shots for yourself. It means accepting mistakes and failures as well as giving yourself credit for all your good work and successes.

Laura's Story: A Tough Responsibility

Laura had never been an especially good student. But her science teacher noticed that she took an interest in the many plants and flowers in the lab. The teacher assigned Laura the responsibility of looking after the plants. She had to make sure they had enough water and sunlight and were returned to the science lab after class use.

At first, Laura was not sure she wanted to be bothered with the extra work. It took more time than she expected. She heard a boy in the science class, Joe, make a remark about how she was trying to be the teacher's pet. The remark made her so mad that she became determined to stick to her new job and do it right. She soon found herself more and more fascinated with the plants. She decided to do her final paper on how plants grow. The teacher noticed her efforts, and her grade went up.

One day several of the biggest, most beautiful plants were missing from the science lab. Laura was furious. Somebody had stolen *her* best plants! Later, a friend told Laura that she had heard three kids in the class say they had taken the plants home. They bragged about the theft.

When you take tough jobs and meet your responsibilities success-
fully, you can take pride in your accomplishments.

Laura's first impulse was to tell the teacher. After all, the plants were her responsibility—it was her duty to make sure they were returned. But she thought about it. She wasn't sure that what her friend said was true, and she was uncomfortable about telling on other students. She decided to ask the three herself.

Laura was nervous because she wasn't very friendly with the three kids. In fact, one of them was Joe, the boy who had whispered "teacher's pet." But Laura asked them anyway, one at a time. She tried not to sound like she was accusing them. One girl seemed really surprised and said she didn't know what Laura was talking about. Laura believed her. The second kid admitted stealing the plants. Laura said, "I think you should put them back. I don't want to get anybody in trouble. Just put them back, and I won't say anything." He agreed, and the next day two of the missing plants were back in the lab.

When she asked Joe, he said, "So what if I took them? It's none of your business. Go ahead and snitch if you want, I'll deny it."

Laura was not sure what to do. She didn't want to be called a snitch. But she didn't want Joe to get away with the theft, either. She thought about reporting him to the teacher. She was angry at Joe and she disliked him. She wanted "her" plants back. But weren't these just selfish reasons? Hadn't she already lived up to her responsibility by trying to get the plants back on her own? But stealing was wrong. She decided to wait a day before doing anything. Decisions can seem clearer after time goes by.

The next day, Laura told the teacher that Joe had refused to return the plants. She didn't mention the other student who had brought the plants back that he had taken. Laura thought that this was the most responsible thing she could do.

Conscience and Decisions

Was Laura right or wrong to tell the teacher about Joe? Should she also have reported the other student? She had to decide that for herself. She followed her conscience. She made the decision based on her beliefs, not based on her anger or dislike for Joe. And she didn't let her personal interest in the plants or her wish to please the science teacher guide her actions. She felt it would be wrong to keep quiet, even though she also felt uncomfortable about snitching. Someone else might have made a different decision.

Rewards and Costs of Responsibility

Laura's story tells us several things about responsibility and integrity. First, accepting responsibility and living up

Developing a new interest, and doing it well, is a great way to build self-esteem.

to it is great for self-esteem and personal growth. Laura's work with the plants made her proud. Her classwork and grades improved, and her new interest made her life a little richer. The teacher placed trust in Laura, and she lived up to it.

Second, responsibility is not easy. Laura had to put time and effort into her job. She also had to do two tough and courageous things. She had to ask the three kids face-to-face about the theft and decide whether or not to tell the teacher about Joe.

Third, integrity means listening to your conscience and doing the right thing, not the easy thing. Laura thought through the *whole* story. She then acted with integrity. She accepted the results of her decision. Joe would call her a snitch, but she knew she had made a decision that she was personally comfortable with. Overall, the experience was good for Laura's self-esteem and her understanding of her own true self.

The problems and questions of normal everyday life demand responsibility and integrity as much as the more extreme problems we talked about in the last chapter.

The most valuable part of healthy self-esteem is knowing and accepting who you really are.

7

ACCEPTING YOUR TRUE SELF

WE HAVE TALKED A LOT ABOUT FOLLOWING YOUR CONSCIENCE, listening to your inner beliefs, and getting to know yourself. But it is not always so easy. What *is* that "true self"? How can I know my inner beliefs? What is all this about accepting myself?

These are the questions that everyone spends a lifetime trying to answer. One of the hardest parts about being a teenager is learning all the *questions*, but it takes many years to learn the answers.

You learn about your true self through the experiences of living. But there are a lot of ways to make that voyage of discovery smoother, richer, less confusing, and more productive. Here are some things to remember:

- Problems and imperfections are part of human nature.
- Everyone has positive and negative sides—both good and bad are part of you and have to be accepted.
- There is no progress without risk, and sometimes risks mean failure—everyone has the right to fail.
- When you give up unhealthy illusions about yourself, you can know your true self.

Chapter Seven

- Accepting yourself and being conceited and smug
  are *not* the same thing.

Imperfections

"My mom drives me crazy," Claire complained to Jean. "She always finds something to be miserable about. If it's not worrying about us, it's nagging herself about all the great projects she'll never get around to. So our house isn't a palace. Who cares? She can never relax and take things as they are."

Maybe Claire is right, and her mother really is unable to accept imperfections and problems. If so, she probably *is* miserable a lot of the time. Claire sees this and thinks it's a shame that her mother feels so bad about herself when she really doesn't have to. Claire doesn't want to look at her own life in the same unhappy way. She is learning to accept her mother's discontent as one of the imperfections in her own life.

Accepting the Positive and Negative within Yourself

"I guess I just have a really bad mean streak," thought Nick. He had another fight with his little sister that ended with his punching and her crying. Now he felt guilty and terrible. "I'm a real slime. There must be something really wrong with me."

Nick is probably not as much of a monster as he fears, and his "mean streak" is probably pretty average. Feeling guilty and worrying about his "bad side" does not solve the problem of fighting with his sister. It would be more helpful if Nick figured out why the fights start and how to avoid them. He should recognize that he *does* have a temper. He should work on controlling it instead of hitting now and feeling guilty later. Nick doesn't want to admit that a good guy like him could have a bad temper. But he has to admit and accept it before he can improve it.

Risk and the Right to Fail

Allison was a fine pianist. She decided that she wanted to transfer from her school to a special music and art high school. Lots of talented kids were competing to get accepted at the school. Allison had a part-time job and was saving money for a vacation. But she gave up her job and other activities to concentrate on practicing for the entrance audition. She was very pleased with her audition performance but very disappointed when she learned that she had not been accepted. "Boy," she said to her friend Nina, "did I waste my time! I should have known I wasn't good enough." "I wouldn't say that," answered Nina. "With all that practicing, you're a better pianist than ever. Keep it up, and you'll get yourself a college scholarship in a couple of years."

We grow and develop by trying new things and pushing our limits. But we won't always be successful when we take risks. Allison sacrificed her job, vacation, and free time to try out for something she wanted. It was a risk. Although she was not accepted at the school, she doesn't have to see the failure as a total defeat. She has gained by the experience, both as a pianist and as a person who understands her own goals and wishes.

Illusions and the True Self

Zack's father was a busy and successful lawyer. He seemed to love the long hours, hectic pace, and wheeling and dealing. Zack grew up expecting to be just as ambitious and successful. He assumed that his parents expected it, too. But as Zack went through school, he found that he was not very outgoing and quick with words. He was more interested in his art classes. He used his imagination. The work was quiet and careful. He was happy with the results. Outside of art class, though, Zack was shy and his grades were not great. He felt like a failure, and he was sure that his father was disappointed in him.

One day when Zack's parents came home from a parent-teacher conference, his father praised him. Even though Zack had barely passed some classes, the art teacher said Zack had a lot of artistic talent and worked

Healthy self-esteem means
having the confidence to
take risks, even if your
attempt does not win you
the first prize.

very hard on his paintings. Zack was surprised to learn that his parents were impressed and supportive.

He started to understand that he didn't have to be just like his father. He worried less about being a failure. He took more pride in what he did well. As his artwork improved, so did his self-confidence. Pretty soon, he felt less shy and stupid. He started to do better in other classes, too. He even felt closer to his parents.

Self-Esteem or Swelled Head?

If self-esteem meant only thinking highly of yourself, Patty would have enough self-esteem to burn. Patty is smart. She figures she'll be a world-famous journalist or maybe a millionaire stockbroker. She's pretty, too. Maybe she'll be a movie actress, instead. Her clothes are chic. She always seems to know about the latest fads a month before anybody else. She has more than her share of dates. Patty knows very well that she is quite a hot item. In fact, Patty is conceited. She treats everybody else as if they're not good enough for her. She's too bored to listen to what other people have to say. She expects the guys she dates to treat her like royalty. Not surprisingly, her boyfriends don't last very long. She doesn't really have a close friend, male or female. Inside, she is lonely. She knows that people don't really like her.

Patty thinks a lot of herself. But she does not have the respect for other people that is so necessary for true self-esteem. Because she does not have respect for others, others don't respect or like her. No matter how proud of herself and outwardly confident she is, if she lacks respect from others, she will be lonely. This will keep her from being truly comfortable with herself.

Trying new things and overcoming your fears are excellent ways to raise your self-confidence.

8

STEPS TOWARD SELF-ESTEEM

IF YOU FEEL THAT YOUR SELF-ESTEEM is not as strong as you'd like it to be, there are many ways to strengthen self-confidence and self-respect. It is important to remember, however, that changing deeply felt attitudes about yourself can be a long and complicated process.

Traps and Roadblocks

First, find ways that low self-esteem trips you up. Do you:

- Let a negative inner voice put you down?
- Let "The Doubts" keep you from taking challenges?
- Assume that you'll fail—expect to fail—and then fail?
- Value yourself for how others see you? How popular you are?
- Follow the pack—even when you disagree?
- Treat others with disrespect? Yourself?
- Set goals you can't reach? Feel dissatisfied with goals you *do* reach?

- Feel as if you're on show for others?
- Think you'll never live up to your parents' expectations?
- Feel like you don't belong anywhere?
- Fear risks? Expect perfection?
- Avoid responsibility because you think you won't live up to it?

Everybody has these feelings at one time or another. The trick is to be able to control and even overcome doubts and to work around them instead of letting them stop you in your tracks.

Battling the Negative Inner Voice

An important step is to do battle with that destructive inner voice, the one that calls you stupid, puts you down, puts "The Doubts" in your mind, and arranges for failure in advance. You must make a planned effort to talk back to the negative inner voice. The next time you call yourself an idiot, cut it off. Say to yourself, "Stop. Right now. I'm not an idiot." If you make a mistake and feel like kicking yourself, cut it off. Tell yourself firmly, "Stop. Everybody makes mistakes. It's not such a big deal."

Of course, talking back to yourself may seem silly at first. You may not be used to an inner voice defending you. The voice that has been putting you down all these years will be stronger and clearer than this new voice. But stick to it. Give it some time and practice. Pretty soon it will feel natural to shut off those destructive, negative thoughts before they make you feel terrible about yourself.

Your Private "A" List

You might try this: In a private notebook or diary, make a list of your strengths and good points. Are you helpful around the house? Write it down. Great at snagging fly balls? Patient with your kid brother? Fastest wrench in auto shop? Write it all down. Don't bother making a list of the *bad* things. You know those by heart already. Your good list is just for you, not for anybody else to see.

Putting Respect into Practice

We talked about how respecting yourself is tied in with respecting others. Put respect into practice. Go out of your way to treat the people around you with kindness. Listen to their feelings. Show them that you value them. You don't have to make a big deal of it. Start off by just being a little more polite to the bus driver. Be a little more understanding of the kid everybody makes fun of. Try being a little more open with your parents and a little better behaved in the classroom. Don't expect anybody to give you a gold star or a pat on the head. If you get into the habit of treating others with respect, you'll start to feel better about yourself, too.

Make sure that other people know that you expect to be treated with respect, too. That means speaking up for yourself. This doesn't mean angry demands, but it does mean explaining your feelings as honestly as you can. Say you have a friend who has always been able to talk you into doing something you don't really want to do. Are you being bullied into it? Maybe it is time to let that friend know that he or she is taking advantage of you. It doesn't have to be a fight or the end of a friendship, if the person is a true friend.

It is often hard to stand up for yourself to a friend. It's even harder to say no to a group or to defend yourself to a parent or teacher. You have a right to state your case when you feel you have been treated unfairly.

Let Yourself Shine

Put these self-esteem ideas to work. You will begin to discover new strengths, new interests, new confidence in yourself. You will feel like trying new things, taking risks, stretching your limits, and growing. You will get to know your "true self."

Let that true self shine. You will discover that treating others with kindness and respect makes your own life richer. Take it one step further. Help others. Do community volunteer work. Read to the elderly, or work with kids in the hospital. Ask your school counselor for suggestions (and see "For Further Reading" for a book on this subject).

Take Risks

If you're feeling a little braver than you used to, maybe it's because you have stopped putting yourself down. You have tried to be aware of your good points, and you have started standing up for yourself. Take that new bravery for a "test drive." Try out for an activity or a sport in school. Get involved with a hobby on your own. Goals will become clearer as you follow your interests. Keep in mind that progress means risk, and risks can mean failure. But remember that failure is not a crime. It happens to everybody. Don't be afraid to try again.

Don't expect changes overnight. It takes time and effort to build up your self-esteem and to learn to defend it. Try to remember that no one else knows you as well as you do. Even if someone says you have no talent, you know that to be untrue. And that's all that matters. Just making the decision to take risks and taking the first steps will make you feel good. You'll be taking responsibility for your life. You'll be in charge.

CONCLUSION

THROUGHOUT THIS BOOK WE HAVE STRESSED the value within every one of us. We have seen the connections between acting with respect and responsibility, discovering our "true selves," and having a feeling of self-esteem. They fit together.

Self-esteem is not a feel-good pill. It is the result of efforts to live your life in a way you can be proud of. It's also what gives you the strength and determination to make those efforts. The more effort you put in, the more self-esteem you gain. You'll be better at choosing and reaching goals. You will understand and live up to your values and beliefs. You can accept responsibilities and find your place in the world. It's a winning circle.

Questions and struggles will continue throughout your life. With self-esteem, you will see them all as part of the rich challenge of being a human being—an imperfect, changing, growing, learning human being.

Glossary: *Explaining New Words*

abuse Deliberately hurting someone you are supposed to care about or care for.

achievement Accomplishment; reaching a goal.

clique A circle of friends that excludes others.

competition A contest in sports or any other activity where participants strive to win or be the best.

conceited Thinking too highly of oneself.

confident Sure of oneself, believing in one's abilities.

conformity Being like everyone else.

conscience The part of us that tells us what is right or wrong.

contradictions A statement or situation that conflicts with another statement or situation.

encouragement Giving support and confidence.

esteem (self-esteem) To consider something or someone valuable.

expectation A belief that something will or should happen; also, a feeling of being obliged to do or be something.

illusion Believing in something that is not real.

integrity Doing what one thinks is morally right.

perfectionist Someone who cannot accept mistakes or failure.

realistic Seeing things as they really are.

responsibility Being accountable for one's actions.

secure Sure of something; without doubts or fears.

status (in a group) The position that someone is in and the prestige that goes with the position.

valedictorian The student selected to speak for the class at graduation, usually the top student.

values The set of beliefs by which one lives; one's understanding of right and wrong; the things that are most important to one.

For Further Reading

Baker, Russell. *Growing Up.* New York: Congdon & Weed, 1982. This memoir of growing up during the Depression of the 1930s, written by a well-known journalist, was an adult best-seller and is not specifically aimed at young people, but it's a wonderful look at how family and society shape a young man's sense of identity and coming of age. Worth a little extra reading effort.

Booher, Dianna Daniels. *Making Friends with Yourself and Other Strangers.* New York: J. Messner, 1982. This book, for teens, mostly deals with friendship, but it also contains good material on self-esteem and self-confidence.

Cohen, Daniel & Susan. *Teenage Stress.* New York: M. Evans & Co., Inc., 1984. A broad-ranging book on many problems causing stress among teenagers, with emphasis on physical and emotional effects of stress and ways of battling stress.

Guy, David. *Second Brother.* New York: New American Library, 1985. Young adult fiction. The story of a boy who feels in the shadow of his older brother, and how he works out his self-esteem problems.

Kramer, Patricia. *Discovering the Real You.* New York: Rosen Publishing Group, 1991. A self-help book for teens.

McFarland, Rhoda. *Coping Through Self-Esteem.* New York: Rosen Publishing Group, 1988. A thorough look at the meaning and importance of self-esteem, with practical advice on how to find and strengthen the self-esteem within you. For teens.

Methabane, Mark. *Kaffir Boy.* New York: Macmillan Publishing Co., 1986. Like *Growing Up,* this is an adult-level memoir. This story of a young black South African learning about life, himself, and his society under apartheid tells us much about the forces that can damage self-esteem and the inner strength that fights for self-esteem.

INDEX

About the Author

Alicia Thomas is a free-lance writer and mother living in Berkeley, California, with special interests in education, child development, and the arts.

Photo Credits and Acknowledgments

Cover Photo: Barbara Kirk
Photos on pages 2, 8, 14, 20, 23, 29, 39, 42, 44, 49, 52: Stuart Rabinowitz; pages 11, 17, 30, 32: Chris Volpe; page 25: Charles Waldron

Design and Production: Blackbirch Graphics, Inc.